Fairways to Parenting

A mentor's guide to developing self-confidence, fostering creativity, and mastering the discipline needed to succeed in sports and life.

Jimmie A. Vincent MS

Fairways to Parenting:
A Mentor's Guide to Developing Self-Confidence, Fostering Creativity, and Mastering the Discipline Needed to Succeed in Sports and Life

© 2024 Jimmie A. Vincent

All rights reserved. No part of this book may be reproduced, stored in a retrieval system, or transmitted in any form or by any means, electronic, mechanical, photocopying, recording, or otherwise, without the prior written permission of the publisher, except in the case of brief quotations embodied in critical articles and reviews.

Published by:
Jimmie A. Vincent MS
www.helpinghoundskids.com

ISBN: 9798323704262

This book is a work of non-fiction. Names, characters, businesses, places, events, and incidents are either the product of the author's imagination or used in a fictitious manner. Any resemblance to actual persons, living or dead, or actual events is purely coincidental.

Cover Design by: Jimmie A. Vinent MS

Printed in the United States of America

First Edition: July 2024

For information about special discounts for bulk purchases, please contact.
www.helpinghoudskids.co

Dedication

This book is dedicated to parents, mentors, coaches, siblings, and caregivers who are committed to guiding youth toward a brighter future. For me, trauma, neglect, and chaos were the norm before my 13th birthday. An extraordinarily traumatic event changed my life's trajectory, teaching me the profound impact of a supportive community.

To Micheline, Mireille, Ricardo (Mo-T), Ozzie, Coach McDonald (Dean Mac), Coach Ray, Mr. Abrams, Mrs. Abrams, Mr. Mullins, Mrs. Hart, Mr. Doraville, Mr. Lampkin, Mr. Butts, Coach Allen, Coach Lutz, Coach Bueno, Coach Watson, Coach Killets, Mr. Pyfrom, The Lovelys, and all who supported me—you are why I do the work that I do. From the bottom of my heart, thank you.

Table of Contents:

	Introduction	7
1.	Setting the Foundation: Building Strong Relationships	12
2.	Embracing the love of the game and life	17
3.	Communication: The key to understanding	21
4.	Patience: Nurturing Growth and Development	26
5.	Resilience: Bouncing Back from Setbacks	31
6.	Navigating Stress and Adversity: Resilience in Golf and Life	35
7.	Discipline: The Path to Consistency and Stress	39
8.	Creativity: Thinking Outside the Box	43
9.	Confidence: Believing in yourself	47
10.	Adaptability: Thriving in Changing Environments	52
11.	Autonomy and Independence: Empowering Your Mental Caddie	56
12.	Gratitude: Cultivating Appreciation and Humility	60

Introduction

Hey there, I'm Jimmie A. Vincent, and I'm thrilled to embark on this journey with you. With a master's in Mental Health Counseling, I've dedicated my life to serving others—both as a mental health professional and as a proud Haitian American father of four amazing kids. Alongside my cherished role as a husband of 14 years, I've also championed causes close to my heart as a passionate community advocate.

In my relentless pursuit of making a difference, I co-founded 10AllIn Inc., a nonprofit that introduces underprivileged youth to the worlds of STEAM and golf-related careers. Here, the "A" in STEAM stands for the arts, emphasizing the critical importance of social and emotional wellness in recognizing each student's unique attributes and preparing them for exciting career paths.

This new chapter in my life started in late 2023 when I decided to leave my full-time healthcare administrator role to focus entirely on our nonprofit. My dedication to family and community has always been a driving force, but another passion fuels my spirit—golf. I love the outdoors, and the golf course is my sanctuary.

So why are we here? This book is a testament to the power of passionate parenting, mentoring, and sports education in shaping our youth's futures. Our mission is clear: to explore effective parenting and mentoring within the realm of golf, integrating the principles of Social and Emotional Learning (SEL). SEL is a cornerstone of our work with students and a guiding force in my personal journey as a father.

What is Social and Emotional Learning (SEL)? Simply put, SEL is the process of developing the essential life skills that help us navigate the world with ease, empathy, and understanding. It's the ability to be aware of our emotions, manage them, and use them to fuel our best selves. SEL is the capacity to form meaningful relationships, communicate effectively, and make responsible decisions.

In short, SEL is the superpower that helps us:

- Recognize and regulate our emotions
- Develop empathy and understanding for others
- Form healthy relationships
- Make informed decisions
- Achieve our goals

By cultivating these skills, we set ourselves up for success in all areas of life - personal, academic, and professional. And, as parents and mentors, we play a vital role in helping our children develop this superpower.

As parents, guardians, mentors, and educators, we all share a common goal—to nurture the potential of the next generation. In our busy lives, it's easy to overlook how sports education can shape character and life skills.

Together, we'll discover the gems of wisdom hidden in the fairways of parenting and mentoring. We'll explore the key principles that guide youth to excel—both on and off the golf course. These principles are actionable strategies we can use daily with the young minds we inspire.

So, let's stand together, ready to explore the parallels of parenting, mentoring, and golf instruction. Let's forge a path for a future generation of bold, resilient, and compassionate leaders—guided by the timeless wisdom in *Fairways to Parenting*. Let's start with the reflection in the mirror.

Parenting from Trauma-A Personal Odyssey

Parenting from Trauma" was my mantra in the early days of parenthood. It reminded me to avoid the shadows of my own upbringing and create a brighter path for my kids. But over time, I realized the phrase had a deeper meaning than I initially thought.

The scars of my childhood still linger, a constant reminder of the trauma I endured. Between birth and age 13, I experienced unimaginable hardship and neglect, with over eight removals from our home due to the treacherous environment. Alcoholism, domestic violence, and squalid living conditions were the norm. But the most indelible mark was left on my soul when, at 13, I walked into a crime scene that would haunt me to this day. My mother, in a fit of rage, grief, hate, envy, revenge or some other motive, had poured scalding hot grease on the man I knew as my father while he slept. The stench of his scalding flesh still lingers in my mind.

Those sleepless nights that followed were filled with a resolve that burned deeper with each passing day. I vowed to create a different world for my future family, one where love, safety, and hope would reign. I promised myself that my children would never suffer as I did, that they would be nurtured, supported, and loved unconditionally. This is what I mean by 'Parenting from Trauma' - breaking free from the shackles of my past to forge a brighter future for my family.

For me, parenting from trauma means more than just avoiding the mistakes of my parents. It means creating a sanctuary where my children can grow, learn, and thrive. It means being the safe haven I never had, the rock that provides unwavering support and guidance. My childhood may have been marked by trauma, but my parenthood is defined by resilience, hope, and determination.

Parenting today isn't just about providing food and shelter. It's about building a rich foundation of experiences and lessons into our children's upbringing. Parenting is an art—a delicate dance between shaping our kids' futures and letting them discover their paths. It's about taking the best of who we are and pouring it into the next generation while fostering their individuality and curiosity. So, my mantra is to no longer "parent from trauma", yet to operate from experience with the desire to create lasting memories that aren't tainted by events similar to those of my past.

But here's the twist: parenting isn't a solo performance. It's a intricate dance, where the rhythm changes with every partner, culture, religion, and economic background that enters the stage. Our childhood experiences, with all their scars and triumphs, also join the choreography. This delicate balance underscores the vital importance of choosing our life partners with intention and care - a crucial consideration that, surprisingly, slips the minds of many. As we embark on this journey, we must remember that our partners, with their unique experiences and perspectives, will shape our parenting approach in profound ways. The harmony or discord we create will have a lasting impact on our children's lives.

Implication for Coaches and Mentors

Enter coaching and mentoring—a realm where guidance and independence blend. Unlike the parent-child dynamic, coaching and mentoring offer a more straightforward relationship. Yet, there's a wealth of opportunity to impart invaluable life lessons beneath the surface.

As coaches and mentors, we can impart wisdom in ways that resonate deeply with our students. By integrating essential principles into activities, we create a space where learning feels effortless and organic. It's a subtle dance of influence—allowing students to absorb insights without feeling the weight of parental advice.

As we navigate parenting from trauma, remember it's not just about shielding our kids from the past—it's about crafting a future filled with resilience, empathy, and potential. In the process, we'll discover the profound beauty in guiding the next generation toward their brightest futures.

From Self Awareness to Responsible Decision Making

As I embarked on this journey of parenting and mentoring, I realized that I needed to start with the most critical foundation of all - myself. I had spent years trying to help others, but I knew that I couldn't truly show up for them until I confronted my own demons. It was time to stop running from my past and start embracing my own healing. In the following chapter, 'Setting the Foundation,' I share my personal journey of self-discovery, from the dark corners of my childhood to the transformative power of mindfulness and introspection. Join me as I explore the essential first steps towards building a stronger, wiser, and more compassionate self - the foundation upon which all meaningful relationships are built.

Chapter 1

Setting the Foundation: Building Strong Relationships

"You have to earn their trust and respect."

Earl Woods

In the journey of parenting and mentoring youth in golf, establishing strong relationships forms the bedrock upon which all further development is built. These relationships serve as the conduit through which guidance, support, and learning flow. Please keep in mind that relationships are not all the same. For example, before attempting to start or maintain a relationship with anyone else, we must have a positive relationship with ourselves. Too often we are extremely hard on ourselves and don't forgive ourselves for the mistakes we have made. If we don't learn to forgive ourselves and maintain a healthy relationship with our inner self, it will be extremely difficult to love the people you are trying to influence. The type of relationship you have with your child, mentee, or student athlete must be one that is conducive to their best interest in the aspect of their overall growth and wellbeing.

Which brings me to my next point, boundaries. Boundaries are a foundational aspect of building and developing healthy relationships. The youth that parents and coaches work with may not know as much about healthy relationships and boundaries. However, we as adults should never allow boundaries to be crossed into friendship, or any other inappropriate adult-child relationship. This should in turn teach youth how to develop and manage relationships with peers and others. This idea not only comes from my personal experiences and professional work, but scholars also study and write about such phenomenon in the youth development space. For example, the Journal on Family Psychology in an article titled "The importance of boundaries in adult-child relationships wrote, "Establishing and maintaining healthy boundaries is crucial in adult-child relationships, as it promotes mutual respect, autonomy, and emotional well-being for both parties involved." (Smith, J., & Johnson, A., 2020).

Building strong relationships with children and youth is paramount for several reasons:

1.	Trust and Comfort: When children feel a strong connection with their parents or mentors, they are more likely to feel safe, secure, and comfortable expressing themselves. This trust forms the foundation for open communication and collaboration.

2.	Emotional Support: Strong relationships provide a support system for children to navigate challenges, setbacks, and triumphs. Knowing they have someone in their corner fosters resilience and emotional well-being.

3.	Role Modeling: Children often emulate the behaviors and attitudes of those they look up to. By establishing positive relationships, parents and mentors can model desirable traits such as empathy, respect, and integrity.

4.	Learning Environment: A strong relationship creates an optimal learning environment where children are receptive to guidance, instruction, and feedback. They are more likely to engage actively in the learning process when they feel connected to their parent or mentor.

5.	Model Boundaries: Healthy boundaries are one of, if not, they most important lessons to teach a child. The dynamic between two people is one that should always be of mutual benefit. However, if as an adult, your intention is for something other than the wellbeing of the child, you should reevaluate your reason for having this relationship.

6.   Be Consistent: Consistency is key to so many aspects of both life and golf. So be consistent in the ways you establish trust, provide support, model healthy behaviors, and present a safe environment for learning,

The process of building trust and rapport in parenting and golf mentoring shares many parallels:

1.   Consistency: Consistency in actions, words, and expectations builds trust over time. Whether on the golf course or at home, children thrive in environments where they know what to expect from their parents or mentors.

2.   Active Listening: Both effective parenting and golf mentoring require active listening. By attentively listening to children's thoughts, concerns, and experiences, parents and mentors demonstrate respect and empathy, laying the groundwork for trust.

3.   Empathy and Understanding: Empathy plays a crucial role in establishing rapport. Parents and mentors who empathize with children's perspectives and emotions forge deeper connections, fostering mutual understanding and trust.

4.   Positive Reinforcement: Encouragement and praise are essential components of building trust and rapport. Recognizing children's efforts and achievements, both on and off the golf course, reinforces their sense of value and worth within the relationship.

To cultivate strong relationships with children and youth, consider implementing the following practical tips:

1.   Spend Quality Time Together: Dedicate time to engage in shared activities, whether it's playing golf, participating in hobbies, or simply having meaningful conversations. Quality time strengthens bonds and creates lasting memories.

2.   Communicate Openly and Honestly: Foster an environment of open communication where children feel comfortable expressing themselves without fear of judgment. Be honest, transparent, and respectful in your interactions.

3.   Show Genuine Interest: Take a genuine interest in children's interests, passions, and concerns. Ask open-ended questions, actively listen to their responses, and validate their feelings and experiences.

4. Be Present and Attentive: Demonstrate your commitment to the relationship by being present both physically and emotionally. Put away distractions, maintain eye contact, and actively engage with children during interactions.

5. Respect Boundaries and Autonomy: Recognize and respect children's boundaries and autonomy. Allow them space to express themselves, make decisions, and learn from their experiences, while offering guidance and support when needed.

6. Set Expectations: Setting expectations are similar to setting goals. In working relationships with youth, it is important to make sure that the youth understand what is expected of them so that they have a clear understanding of what they are aspiring to. How you get there, is what you get to have fun creating.

By prioritizing the establishment of strong relationships, parents and mentors lay the groundwork for positive growth, development, and success in both golf and life. These connections serve as the cornerstone upon which all other principles of Fairways to Parenting are built. This book is meant to be intentional in its suggestions. The expectation is that we as parents take heed to this material, to do our part in raising happy, healthy, and resilient children.

Reflection Statement: *Building strong relationships is the foundation for a supportive and nurturing environment, teaching our children the importance of trust, communication, and mutual respect.*

Questions:

- *How do you actively work to strengthen your relationships with family, friends, and colleagues, and how can you model this for your child?*

- *Reflect on a time when you built a strong relationship from the ground up. What steps did you take, and how can you share these practices with your child?*

Chapter 2

Embracing the Love of the Game and Life

"Success in this game depends less on strength of body than strength of mind and character."

Arnold Palmer

Love is a powerful force that enriches both the game of golf and the journey of life. As adults, we may or may not understand the importance of "loving what you do and doing what you love." But that's okay. This book is designed to help you understand that, if you are passionate about what you do, then you are not working at all. A love of life, golf, or anything else allows for the development of passion, joy, and purpose into our experiences, creating deep connections and meaningful relationships. In building a foundation with my children, I could not be hypocritical and push my children to follow their dreams and do what they love, if me as their example was following a daily routine that I did not absolutely love. Rewardingly, this is how I found myself doing the work that I do. I followed a passion that most thought I was insane for following. I admit that it's been a bit frightening, but I am proud to say that I can look at myself in the mirror and know that I love what I do.

This chapter explores the intertwined concepts of love for the game of golf and love for life, highlighting their similarities, benefits, and how they complement each other in shaping our attitudes, behaviors, and outlook on the world. So, as you get through this chapter. I challenge you to ask yourself the following question. "If I could do something every single day for the rest of my life, and not get paid, what would that be?" For me the answer would hands down be; building communities by developing youth (starting with my own kids), and playing golf. What about you?

Exploring the Essence of Love: Love lies at the heart of both the game of golf and life itself:

1. In Golf: The love of the game fuels golfers' passion for the sport, driving them to pursue excellence, overcome challenges, and savor every moment on the course. It fosters camaraderie, sportsmanship, and a sense of belonging within the golfing community.

2. In Life: Love is the foundation of our relationships, experiences, and aspirations in life. It inspires us to cherish our connections with others, embrace new opportunities, and find meaning and fulfillment in our journey.

3. Combined: My love for my family, my community, and future generations allow a sport in which I have a deep affinity for to be a driving force in my life. For you, this might look very different. However, you owe it to yourself as a parent, educator, or mentor to see to it that the youth you work with are able to find their passion in life. It won't hurt if there is a sport, or physical activity attached to it.

Understanding the Intersection: The love of the game and love of life intersect in profound ways:

1. Shared Joy: Both golf and life offer moments of joy, triumph, and camaraderie that are made even sweeter when shared with others who share our passion and enthusiasm.

2. Resilience and Adaptability: Love instills resilience and adaptability, empowering us to bounce back from setbacks, face challenges with courage, and embrace change with optimism and determination.

3. Appreciation and Gratitude: Love cultivates appreciation and gratitude for the beauty, experiences, and relationships that enrich our

lives, encouraging us to savor each moment and express thanks for the blessings we encounter.

Nurturing Love on the Golf Course and Beyond: Strategies for nurturing love on the golf course and in life include:

1. Embrace the Journey: Encourage golfers and individuals to embrace the journey of improvement and growth, recognizing that each step forward, whether on the course or in life, is a testament to their love for the game and their commitment to personal development.

2. Cultivate Connection: Foster connections and relationships with fellow golfers and members of the community, sharing experiences, insights, and encouragement that deepen our appreciation for the game and enrich our lives.

3. Practice Gratitude: Cultivate gratitude for the opportunities, experiences, and relationships that bring joy and fulfillment to our lives, taking time to reflect on the blessings we encounter both on and off the golf course.

Embracing the love of the game and love of life is a process of discovery, growth, and fulfillment. By nurturing our passion for golf and cherishing the experiences and connections that enrich our lives, we cultivate a deep sense of appreciation, joy, and meaning that resonates both on and off the course. Let us continue to celebrate the love that fuels our journey, inspiring us to play the game of golf and live our lives with passion, purpose, and gratitude.

Reflection Statement: *Embracing the love of the game and life means finding joy and passion in what we do, teaching our children to pursue their interests wholeheartedly.* **Questions:**

- *How can you show your enthusiasm for life and activities to inspire your child?*

- *Reflect on a time when your passion for an activity positively influenced your child's interest. What happened?*

_____
_____

Chapter 3

Communication: The Key to Understanding

"Success in this game depends less on strength in the body than strength of mind and character."

Arnold Palmer

Effective communication serves as the cornerstone of successful parenting, mentoring, and teaching in golf. I have heard it stated that upwards of 70-90% of all communication is nonverbal. While that number is up for debate, the fact remains that as parents, educator, and mentors, it is our obligation to understand our youth as best we can. We can't effectively do this if we don't consider nonverbal cues. When I worked as a therapist, I was held to a standard of observing the entire person as part of my assessment of their concerns. In fact, according to an article by the National Institutes of Health (2010) on nonverbal communication in psychology, clients' "interaction with the environment" was one of the nonverbal cues I had to be aware of in order to do effective work. Similarly, we have to keep in mind that just because something isn't said, doesn't mean that it isn't felt or implied.

It is through communication that understanding, connection, and growth are facilitated. This chapter delves into the pivotal role of communication in fostering meaningful relationships, imparting lessons, and shaping values both on and off the golf course.

Communication in parenting and mentoring serves several crucial functions:

1. Building Trust and Rapport: Clear, honest communication fosters trust and rapport between parents/mentors and children/youth. It creates an environment where individuals feel valued, heard, and understood.

2. Conveying Guidance and Instruction: Effective communication enables parents and mentors to convey guidance, instruction, and feedback in a manner that is clear, concise, and supportive. It empowers children and youth to learn and grow from the wisdom imparted to them.

3. Nurturing Emotional Connection: Communication provides a platform for expressing emotions, feelings, and experiences. Through open dialogue, parents and mentors can nurture emotional connection, empathy, and understanding within their relationships.

4. Fostering Environments of Healthy Engagement and Safe Spaces: Understanding your child or student is one of the best ways to have breakthroughs and maintain healthy connections with them. If a person doesn't feel understood, it is unlikely that they will be open to you about what's happening in their life. Take the time and do the work necessary to understand your child or young athlete. Operate from a place of understanding, not assumptions.

Effective communication strategies play a pivotal role in conveying lessons and values through golf and everyday life:

1. Use Clear and Concise Language: Communicate messages using language that is easy to understand and free from ambiguity. This ensures that children and youth grasp the intended lessons and values clearly.

2. Lead by Example: Model effective communication behaviors in your interactions with children and youth. Demonstrate active listening, empathy, and respect, serving as a positive example for them to emulate.

3. Encourage Two-Way Dialogue: Foster open, two-way communication where children and youth feel comfortable expressing their thoughts, questions, and concerns. Encourage active participation and dialogue to deepen understanding and connection.

4.   Incorporate Visual Aids and Demonstrations: In golf instruction, as well as in everyday life, utilize visual aids, demonstrations, and hands-on activities to reinforce lessons and values. Visual learning enhances comprehension and retention.

Challenges in communication may arise due to various factors such as differences in communication styles, generational gaps, or emotional barriers. To overcome these challenges:

1.   Practice Active Listening: Cultivate the habit of active listening, wherein you focus on understanding the speaker's perspective without interrupting or formulating responses prematurely.

2.   Foster Empathy and Understanding: Empathize with the emotions and experiences of children and youth, seeking to understand their viewpoint and feelings. Validate their experiences and demonstrate empathy in your communication.

3.   Adapt Communication Styles: Recognize and adapt your communication style to suit the preferences and needs of children and youth. Flexibility in communication enhances receptivity and understanding.

To establish a foundation for teaching effective communication:

1.   Start Early: Begin teaching communication skills from a young age, incorporating age-appropriate language and activities to develop foundational communication skills.

2.   Emphasize Emotional Expression: Encourage children and youth to express their thoughts, emotions, and feelings openly and honestly. Provide a safe and supportive environment for them to share their innermost thoughts.

3.   Practice Communication Exercises: Engage in communication exercises and activities that promote active listening, empathy, and effective expression. Role-playing scenarios, reflective journaling, and group discussions are effective tools for honing communication skills.

By prioritizing effective communication, parents and mentors lay the groundwork for fostering understanding, connection, and growth in children and youth, both on the golf course and in everyday life. Remember that if a child does not or chooses not to verbalize as their primary way of communicating, pay attention to their actions, behaviors, body language, eye contact and facial expressions.

Reflection Statement: *Effective communication is essential for understanding and connecting with others, helping our children develop strong interpersonal skills.* **Questions:**

- *How do you model active listening and clear communication for your child?*

- *Think of a recent misunderstanding. How could better communication have improved the situation?*

_____
_____
_____
_____
_____
_____
_____
_____
_____
_____
_____
_____
_____
_____
_____
_____
_____
_____
_____
_____
_____
_____

Chapter 4

Patience: Nurturing Growth and Development

"Success is not determined by how many times you fall, but by how many times you get back up."

Ricky Fowler

Patience is not merely the ability to wait, but the capacity to maintain a positive attitude while waiting. In parenting and golf instruction, patience is a fundamental virtue that nurtures growth and development. This chapter explores the significance of patience in fostering resilience, skill development, and character building, both on and off the golf course. How we exhibit patience with our children, as well as with other adult-child relationships sets the stage for fostering optimal outcomes in future situations. This is highlighted by Shonkoff and Phillips (2000), who wrote "Effective nurturing environments are characterized by warmth, responsiveness, and sensitivity to individual differences, and they provide children with opportunities for exploration, learning, and skill development."

1. Resilience: Patience cultivates resilience by teaching individuals to endure setbacks, challenges, and obstacles with grace and composure. It

instills the belief that progress takes time and effort, fostering resilience in the face of adversity.

2. Skill Development: In golf instruction, patience is essential for skill development. It encourages learners to persist through the learning curve, mastering techniques and refining their game over time.

3. Character Building: Patience is integral to character building, shaping individuals' attitudes, behaviors, and outlook on life. It promotes virtues such as perseverance, tolerance, and self-discipline, laying the foundation for personal and moral growth.

While patience is a virtue worth cultivating, it is not without its challenges:

1. Instant Gratification Culture: In today's fast-paced society, the culture of instant gratification can make patience seem increasingly elusive. The desire for immediate results often clashes with the reality of gradual progress and development.

2. Frustration and Impatience: Frustration and impatience are natural responses to delays, setbacks, and uncertainties. Learning to manage these emotions is a crucial aspect of mastering patience.

3. Persistence and Perseverance: Developing patience requires persistent effort and perseverance. It involves consciously choosing to respond with patience in the face of frustration or impatience.

Wisdom is essential for cultivating patience:

1. Understanding the Nature of Time: Wisdom entails recognizing that growth, progress, and achievement unfold over time. It involves embracing the journey rather than fixating solely on the destination.

2. Acceptance of Impermanence: Wisdom involves accepting the impermanent nature of life and acknowledging that change takes time. It encourages individuals to cultivate patience amidst uncertainty and flux.

Self-awareness is key to recognizing and cultivating patience:

1. Mindfulness: Practicing mindfulness enables individuals to observe their thoughts, emotions, and reactions without judgment. It fosters awareness of one's impatience and provides the opportunity to choose a patient response.

2. Reflection and Self-Assessment: Engaging in regular reflection and self-assessment allows individuals to evaluate their level of patience and identify areas for improvement. It promotes introspection and personal growth. Both of which are positive qualities we want our youth to gather from our actions and behaviors.

Patience contributes to skill development and character building in various ways:

1. Skill Development: In golf instruction, patience allows learners to persist through the process of learning new techniques, refining their skills, and mastering the intricacies of the game. It fosters perseverance and dedication, leading to continuous improvement.

2. Character Building: Patience cultivates virtues such as resilience, self-discipline, and humility, which are integral to character building. It teaches individuals to approach challenges with determination, grace, and a positive attitude, shaping their character and outlook on life.

Patience is closely linked to happiness and a broader perspective:

1. Cultivating Contentment: Patience enables individuals to find contentment and fulfillment in the present moment rather than constantly striving for future goals or outcomes. It fosters gratitude for what is, rather than longing for what could be.

2. Embracing Diversity of Experience: Patience allows individuals to embrace the diversity of human experience, recognizing that everyone progresses at their own pace. It promotes empathy, understanding, and acceptance of different perspectives and timelines.

Strategies for cultivating patience in oneself and in young learners. To cultivate patience in oneself and in young learners, consider the following strategies:

1. Practice Mindfulness: Incorporate mindfulness practices such as deep breathing, meditation, or yoga into daily routines to cultivate patience and present-moment awareness.

2. Set Realistic Expectations: Encourage realistic expectations and goals, emphasizing that growth and progress take time and effort. Help learners understand that setbacks and challenges are natural parts of the learning process.

3. Foster a Growth Mindset: Cultivate a growth mindset by reframing setbacks and failures as opportunities for learning and growth. Encourage perseverance, resilience, and a positive attitude towards challenges.

4. Model Patience: Lead by example by modeling patience in your own actions, reactions, and interactions with others. Demonstrate resilience, perseverance, and a positive attitude in the face of adversity.

By prioritizing patience, parents, mentors, and golf instructors lay the foundation for resilience, skill development, and character building in themselves and in young learners. Patience serves as a guiding principle that fosters growth, understanding, and happiness both on and off the golf course. If these are things you seek in life, then hold on to these words by Jack Nicholas from the Mind Training (n.d.) website which states "Stay patient and persistent; good things come to those who work for it."

Reflection Statement: *Patience is crucial for nurturing growth and development, teaching our children the value of persistence and gradual progress.* **Questions:**

- *How can you demonstrate patience in your daily interactions with your child?*
- *Describe a situation where patience led to a positive outcome for your child's development.*

_____
_____
_____
_____
_____
_____
_____
_____
_____
_____
_____
_____

Chapter 5

Resilience: Bouncing Back from Setbacks

"Challenges are what make life interesting; overcoming them is what makes it meaningful."

Jack Nicholas

Resilience is the capacity to bounce back from adversity, to adapt positively in the face of challenges, and to thrive despite life's inevitable setbacks. In childhood, life, and on the golf course, resilience plays a vital role in navigating difficulties and achieving success. While resiliency is true to exist in the child population. We must be careful to not take for granted how much a child can "bounce back from", before being permanently traumatized. In fact, "Resilience is not just about bouncing back from adversity; it's about adopting, growing, and thriving despite the challenges. It's the capacity to harness inner strengths and external resources to overcome obstacles and emerge stronger." (Masten, 2008) This chapter explores the importance of resilience, its role in developing adaptability to trauma, negative life events, and other stressors, and offers techniques for building resilience in children and youth.

Resilience is crucial for facing challenges in childhood, life, and golf:

1. Childhood: Resilience enables children to cope with adversity, such as family conflicts, academic struggles, or peer pressure. It equips them with the skills and mindset needed to navigate challenges and setbacks effectively.

2. Life: In adulthood, resilience allows individuals to withstand life's inevitable ups and downs, such as job loss, relationship difficulties, or health issues. It fosters the ability to bounce back from setbacks and pursue goals with determination and optimism.

3. Golf: On the golf course, resilience is essential for maintaining composure in the face of poor performance, unfavorable conditions, or unexpected obstacles. It enables golfers to rebound from setbacks, stay focused on their game, and perform at their best.

Resilience plays a critical role in developing adaptability to trauma, negative life events, and other stressors:

1. Trauma: Resilience helps individuals cope with traumatic experiences, such as loss, abuse, or natural disasters, by promoting emotional regulation, problem-solving skills, and social support networks.

2. Negative Life Events: Resilience enables individuals to navigate negative life events, such as job loss, financial hardship, or relationship breakdowns, with resilience and optimism. It fosters the belief that setbacks are temporary and can be overcome with time and effort.

3. Other Stressors: Resilience equips individuals with the tools to cope with everyday stressors, such as deadlines, conflicts, or setbacks, by promoting adaptive coping strategies, positive thinking, and self-care practices.

Resilience is developed through both parenting and the challenges encountered in golf:

1. Parenting: Parents play a crucial role in fostering resilience in children by providing love, support, and guidance, encouraging autonomy, problem-solving skills, and emotional regulation, and modeling resilient behaviors and attitudes.

2. Golf: The ups and downs of golf provide opportunities for developing resilience by teaching golfers to cope with adversity, manage

frustration, and maintain focus and composure under pressure. Each round offers valuable lessons in resilience and mental toughness.

Techniques for building resilience in children and youth include:

1. Foster Positive Relationships: Cultivate strong, supportive relationships with children and youth, providing a safe and nurturing environment where they feel valued, heard, and supported.

2. Encourage Problem-Solving Skills: Teach children and youth effective problem-solving skills, such as breaking problems into manageable steps, brainstorming solutions, and seeking help when needed.

3. Promote Emotional Regulation: Help children and youth develop emotional regulation skills, such as recognizing and expressing emotions, coping with stress, and practicing relaxation techniques like deep breathing or mindfulness.

Ideals of self-management to promote resilience include:

1. Self-Awareness: Encourage children and youth to develop self-awareness by reflecting on their thoughts, feelings, and behaviors, and identifying areas for growth and improvement.

2. Goal Setting: Teach children and youth to set realistic goals, both in golf and in life, and to develop action plans for achieving them. Goal setting fosters motivation, perseverance, and a sense of accomplishment.

3. Resilient Thinking: Promote resilient thinking by challenging negative self-talk, reframing setbacks as opportunities for growth, and maintaining a positive outlook even in the face of adversity.

By prioritizing resilience, parents, mentors, and golf instructors empower children and youth to navigate life's challenges with confidence, optimism, and determination. Resilience serves as a foundation for success and well-being, both on and off the golf course, enabling individuals to bounce back from setbacks and thrive in the face of adversity. Or as described in the text "The resilience paradox, "In the face of adversity, resilient children demonstrate remarkable flexibility and resourcefulness. They possess a sense of agency and optimism, viewing challenges as opportunities for growth rather than insurmountable barriers. Through supportive relationships and a nurturing environment, children can cultivate resilience and thrive despite adverse circumstances." (Bonanno, 2019)

Reflection Statement: *Resilience helps us bounce back from setbacks, showing our children how to overcome challenges with determination and a positive mindset.* **Questions:**

- *How do you handle setbacks, and how can you teach these strategies to your child?*
- *Reflect on a time when your child faced a challenge. How did you support them in developing resilience?*

Chapter 6

Navigating Stress and Adversity: Resilience in Golf and Life

"Tiger...your training is over. You've got it. I promise you that you'll never meet another person as mentally tough as you."

Earl Woods

Introduction to Navigating Stress: Stress and adversity are inevitable aspects of both the game of golf and the journey of life. How we navigate and overcome these challenges can profoundly impact our well-being, performance, and personal growth. As you will discover below, "Effective stress management in youth involves a combination of developing coping strategies, fostering resilience, and creating supportive environments. By teaching young individuals mindfulness techniques, emotional regulation skills, and problem-solving abilities, we can empower them to navigate stressors more effectively and build the foundation for lifelong well-being." (Jones & Phillips, 2022) In this chapter, we will explore strategies for building resilience in the face of stress and adversity, drawing parallels between the demands of golf and the challenges of life, and offering practical techniques for enhancing mental toughness and emotional well-being.

Understanding the Impact of Stress: Stress can have significant effects on both golfers and individuals in various aspects of life:

1.   In Golf: Stress can manifest as performance anxiety, pressure to perform, or frustration with setbacks on the golf course. It can impair focus, decision-making, and confidence, ultimately affecting one's ability to play at their best.

2.   In Life: Stressors in life, such as work deadlines, relationship conflicts, or health concerns, can contribute to chronic stress, leading to physical and emotional strain, decreased resilience, and impaired overall well-being.

Recognizing the Effects of Toxic Stress on Children: Children exposed to toxic stress may exhibit a range of challenges, including:

1.   Poorly Developed Executive Functioning: Toxic stress can impair the development of executive functioning skills, such as planning, problem-solving, and decision-making, which are essential for success in academics, relationships, and life.

2.   Lack of Self-Regulation and Self-Reflection: Children may struggle with self-regulation and self-reflection, finding it difficult to manage their emotions, behaviors, and impulses in various situations.

3.   Reduced Impulse Control: Toxic stress can compromise impulse control, leading to impulsive behaviors, poor decision-making, and difficulties in social interactions and academic settings.

Building Resilience in Golf and Life: Strategies for building resilience in the face of stress and adversity include:

1.   Mindfulness and Relaxation Techniques: Teach golfers and individuals mindfulness and relaxation techniques, such as deep breathing, visualization, or progressive muscle relaxation, to help manage stress, calm the mind, and enhance focus and performance.

2.   Cognitive Restructuring: Encourage golfers and individuals to challenge negative thought patterns and beliefs that contribute to stress and anxiety, replacing them with more adaptive and empowering perspectives.

3.   Goal Setting and Planning: Assist golfers and individuals in setting realistic goals and developing action plans for achieving them, breaking down tasks into manageable steps and celebrating progress along the way.

4.   Social Support and Connection: Foster a sense of community and support among golfers and individuals, encouraging open communication, empathy, and mutual encouragement during times of stress and adversity.

Navigating stress and adversity is a universal challenge that golfers and individuals encounter both on and off the course. By equipping ourselves with resilience-building strategies and fostering a supportive community, we can navigate life's challenges with greater confidence, composure, and well-being. Let us embrace the opportunities for growth and learning that arise from adversity, recognizing that our capacity to overcome challenges ultimately strengthens our resilience and deepens our appreciation for the game of golf and the journey of life.

The task of navigating stress at young ages can be a difficult one. This is why it is a good idea for parents, mentors, and couches should be equipped to understand and adequately deal with the outcome of youth being faced with some of the new and complex stressors that exist in the digital age. In our capacity, we must prioritize "Encouraging healthy lifestyle habits, promoting positive social connections, and providing access to mental health support are crucial in equipping young people with the tools they need to manage stress effectively and thrive in today's complex world." (Smith et al., 2021)

Reflection Statement: *Navigating stress and adversity builds resilience, teaching our children to stay strong and focused under pressure.* **Questions:**

- *What strategies do you use to manage stress that you can share with your child?*

- *Describe a moment of adversity you faced together and how you both overcame it.*

Chapter 7

Discipline: The Path to Consistency and Success

"Stay focused, stay disciplined, and stay dedicated to your craft."

Jack Nicklas

Discipline is the cornerstone of achieving goals, mastering skills, and fostering personal growth. It encompasses self-control, comprehension of consequences, and accepting responsibility for one's actions. In both parenting and the practice of golf, discipline plays a crucial role in shaping behavior, instilling values, and cultivating success. This chapter explores the multifaceted role of discipline and provides practical methods for teaching discipline and self-control to young people, while also guiding them in managing their feelings and behaviors effectively.

Discipline is essential for various aspects of personal development:

1. Achieving Goals: Discipline enables individuals to set goals, stay focused, and take consistent action towards their objectives. It instills the persistence and dedication needed to overcome obstacles and achieve success.

2. Mastering Skills: Discipline is integral to skill development, as it requires consistent practice, effort, and attention to detail. It fosters the commitment and perseverance needed to master complex tasks and excel in one's endeavors.

3.   Developing Self-Control: Discipline cultivates self-control by teaching individuals to regulate their thoughts, emotions, and behaviors. It empowers individuals to make conscious choices and resist impulsive actions, even in challenging situations.

4.   Comprehension of Consequences: Discipline promotes an understanding of cause and effect, helping individuals recognize the consequences of their actions. It encourages thoughtful decision-making and responsible behavior by considering the potential outcomes of one's choices.

5.   Accepting Responsibility for Actions: Discipline fosters accountability by encouraging individuals to take ownership of their actions and their consequences. It promotes honesty, integrity, and the willingness to learn from mistakes and grow as a person.

Discipline is instilled through parenting and the practice of golf in various ways:

1.   Parenting: Parents play a vital role in modeling and teaching discipline to their children. They establish clear expectations, boundaries, and consequences for behavior and provide consistent guidance and support in enforcing rules and promoting accountability.

2.   Golf Practice: The discipline required for golf practice teaches players valuable life lessons in perseverance, patience, and self-control. Golfers learn to adhere to a routine, maintain focus, and regulate their emotions, enhancing their performance on the course and in other areas of life.

Provide Practical Methods for Teaching Discipline and Self-Control to Young People, While Also Teaching Them How to Manage Both Their Feelings and Behaviors:

Practical methods for teaching discipline and self-control to young people include:

1.   Establish Clear Expectations and Consequences: Set clear expectations for behavior and communicate the consequences of both positive and negative actions. Consistency is key in enforcing rules and holding young people accountable for their behavior.

2. Encourage Goal Setting: Help young people set realistic goals and develop action plans for achieving them. Break goals down into manageable steps and celebrate progress along the way to reinforce discipline and motivation.

3. Teach Emotional Regulation Techniques: Teach young people strategies for managing their emotions, such as deep breathing, mindfulness, and positive self-talk. Encourage them to express their feelings in healthy ways and seek support when needed.

4. Foster Self-Reflection and Problem-Solving Skills: Encourage young people to reflect on their behavior and its impact on themselves and others. Teach them problem-solving skills to address challenges constructively and learn from mistakes.

5. Provide Positive Reinforcement: Recognize and reward young people for demonstrating discipline, self-control, and responsible behavior. Praise their efforts and achievements to reinforce positive habits and attitudes.

By prioritizing discipline and self-control, parents, mentors, and golf instructors empower young people to achieve their goals, master skills, and navigate life's challenges with resilience and responsibility. Discipline serves as a guiding principle that fosters consistency, success, and personal growth, both on and off the golf course. In fact, Tiger Woods, one of the best to ever play the game said, "It's not always easy to be motivated and disciplined, but that's what separates the good players from the great players." Mind Training (n.d)

Reflection Statement: *Discipline is the foundation of consistency and success, guiding our children to develop self-control and achieve their goals.*
Questions:

- *How do you maintain discipline in your life, and how can you instill this value in your child?*
- *Think of a time when discipline led to success for you or your child. What was the result?*

Chapter 8

Creativity: Thinking Outside the Box

"Winners see what they want. Losers see what they don't."

Moe Norman

Creativity is the ability to think outside the box, to innovate, and to approach problems with fresh perspectives. In both parenting and golf, creativity plays a crucial role in problem-solving, skill development, and personal growth. According to The Journal of Child Psychology "Creativity and imagination play a crucial role in child development, fostering cognitive, emotional, and social skills. Through imaginative play and creative expression, children explore the world around them, develop problem-solving abilities, and cultivate a sense of innovation that lays the foundation for future success." (Johnson, E., & Smith, J., 2018). This chapter explores the connection between creativity and problem-solving, the relationship between imagination and creativity, the benefits of fostering creativity in children and youth, and offers strategies for encouraging imaginative thinking on and off the golf course.

Creativity and problem-solving are closely intertwined in parenting and golf:

1.   Parenting: Creative problem-solving enables parents to navigate challenges, conflicts, and obstacles in raising children. It involves thinking

outside the box, exploring alternative solutions, and adapting strategies to meet the unique needs of each child.

2. Golf: In golf, creativity is essential for adapting to changing course conditions, overcoming obstacles, and developing effective strategies for success. Creative golfers approach each shot with innovative techniques and imaginative problem-solving skills, enhancing their performance on the course.

Imagination is the fuel that powers creativity, serving as a wellspring of ideas, possibilities, and inspiration:

1. Generating Ideas: Imagination stimulates the generation of new ideas and concepts, allowing individuals to explore endless possibilities and envision innovative solutions to problems.

2. Encouraging Exploration: Imagination encourages curiosity and exploration, motivating individuals to seek out new experiences, perspectives, and opportunities for growth.

3. Inspiring Innovation: Imagination fuels innovation by sparking creativity, fostering a willingness to experiment, take risks, and push the boundaries of conventional thinking.

Fostering creativity and encouraging imagination in children and youth offers numerous benefits:

1. Enhances Problem-Solving Skills: Creative thinking encourages flexible, innovative problem-solving approaches, empowering children and youth to tackle challenges with confidence and resourcefulness.

2. Stimulates Cognitive Development: Engaging in imaginative activities stimulates cognitive development, fostering critical thinking, abstract reasoning, and mental flexibility.

3. Fosters Resilience and Adaptability: Creativity fosters resilience and adaptability by teaching children and youth to think creatively, adapt to change, and find innovative solutions to setbacks and obstacles.

4. Promotes Self-Expression and Confidence: Encouraging creativity and imagination promotes self-expression and confidence, empowering children and youth to express themselves authentically and pursue their passions with enthusiasm and self-assurance.

Strategies for encouraging imaginative thinking on and off the golf course include:

1. Encourage Play and Exploration: Provide opportunities for children and youth to engage in unstructured play and exploration, allowing them to unleash their imagination and creativity in a supportive environment.

2. Foster a Growth Mindset: Cultivate a growth mindset by praising effort, perseverance, and creativity rather than focusing solely on outcomes or performance. Encourage children and youth to embrace challenges, learn from failures, and persist in the face of setbacks.

3. Provide Open-Ended Activities: Offer open-ended activities and projects that allow children and youth to exercise their creativity and imagination, such as art projects, storytelling, or designing their own golf course holes.

4. Embrace Failure as a Learning Opportunity: Encourage children and youth to embrace failure as a natural part of the creative process, emphasizing that mistakes and setbacks are opportunities for learning, growth, and innovation.

By prioritizing creativity and imagination, parents, mentors, and golf instructors empower children and youth to approach challenges with curiosity, innovation, and enthusiasm. Creativity serves as a catalyst for problem-solving, skill development, and personal growth, both on and off the golf course, fostering a lifelong love of learning and exploration.

Reflection Statement: *Creativity encourages thinking outside the box, inspiring our children to approach problems with innovative solutions and fresh perspectives.* **Questions:**

- *How do you nurture creativity in your child's activities and learning?*
- *Recall a situation where your creative thinking led to a successful outcome. How can you encourage your child to think similarly?*

Chapter 9

Confidence: Believing in Yourself

"Sometimes the biggest problem is in your head. You've got to believe."

Jack Nicholas

Confidence is the belief in one's abilities, strengths, and worth. In both sports and life, self-confidence plays a pivotal role in performance, achievement, and well-being. This chapter explores the importance of self-confidence, identifies confidence destroyers, discusses strategies for building confidence in young people through positive reinforcement and support, and provides techniques for nurturing a strong sense of self-belief in children through structured adversity and "outside the box" thinking.

For those who are religious, it's understood that faith forms the bedrock of any belief system you adhere to. Take, for instance, the belief in a deity that eludes our physical senses—sight, touch, taste, smell, or hearing—in our daily lives. Despite lacking tangible evidence, you maintain unwavering faith in the existence of your god. To you, your deity is as tangible as the pages carrying these words. This unwavering belief extends beyond religion; it's pivotal in achieving personal goals. Whether it's embarking on parenthood with a firm belief in your aspirations or battling self-doubt, the power of belief is undeniable. Self-doubt, in particular, has the detrimental ability to strip away not only our present possessions but also our potential future accomplishments. It underscores the necessity of instilling a sense of belief in our youth—encouraging them to aspire to who they wish to be and what they wish to achieve. Without belief, the vibrant pallet of thoughts, emotions, and experiences associated with the life we envision will remains out of reach.

Self-confidence is essential for success and fulfillment in both sports and life:

1.   Sports: In sports, self-confidence is a key predictor of performance, influencing athletes' motivation, persistence, and resilience. Confident athletes approach challenges with optimism, determination, and a belief in their ability to succeed.

2.   Life: In life, self-confidence is equally crucial for achieving goals, overcoming obstacles, and thriving in various domains such as academics, career, and relationships. Confident individuals exhibit assertiveness, resilience, and a positive outlook, enhancing their overall well-being and success.

Several factors can undermine confidence:

1.   Negative Self-Talk: Negative self-talk, such as self-doubt, criticism, or comparison to others, can erode confidence and undermine belief in one's abilities.

2.   Fear of Failure: Fear of failure can paralyze individuals, preventing them from taking risks, pursuing goals, and stepping outside their comfort zone.

3.   Lack of Support: Lack of support from parents, mentors, or peers can diminish confidence, leaving individuals feeling unsupported and undervalued.

4.   Perfectionism: Perfectionism can sabotage confidence by setting unrealistic standards and expectations, leading to constant self-criticism and dissatisfaction.

Building confidence in young people requires positive reinforcement and support:

1. Encourage Effort and Progress: Praise effort, persistence, and progress rather than focusing solely on outcomes or achievements. Celebrate small victories and milestones to reinforce confidence and motivation.

2. Provide Constructive Feedback: Offer specific, constructive feedback that highlights strengths, identifies areas for improvement, and encourages growth and development.

3. Foster a Supportive Environment: Create a supportive environment where young people feel valued, respected, and encouraged to take risks and pursue their passions. Provide opportunities for collaboration, mentorship, and peer support.

Nurturing self-belief in children through structured adversity involves:

1. Setting Achievable Challenges: Design challenges and tasks that are challenging yet attainable for children, allowing them to experience success and build confidence gradually.

2. Allowing for Failure: Permit children to fail in their attempts, emphasizing that setbacks are opportunities for learning and growth. Encourage resilience and perseverance in the face of adversity.

3. Encouraging "Outside the Box" Thinking: Foster creativity and innovation by encouraging children to approach challenges with "outside the box" thinking. Encourage experimentation, exploration, and unconventional problem-solving strategies.

Arrange challenges that children can overcome, while also fostering resilience and creativity:

1. Create Problem-Solving Scenarios: Present children with real-life scenarios or puzzles that require creative problem-solving and critical thinking skills. Encourage them to brainstorm multiple solutions and explore unconventional approaches.

2. Emphasize Process Over Outcome: Shift the focus from the end result to the process of problem-solving and learning. Encourage children to reflect on their strategies, evaluate their progress, and adapt their approach as needed.

3.   Provide Supportive Guidance: Offer guidance, encouragement, and support as children navigate challenges and setbacks. Be a source of inspiration and motivation, fostering a belief in their ability to overcome obstacles and succeed.

By placing emphasis on positive reinforcement, encouragement, and introducing controlled challenges, parents, mentors, and golf instructors empower young individuals to cultivate self-assurance, resilience, and belief in their capabilities. Confidence forms the bedrock for achievements, both on and off the golf course, enabling children to pursue their aspirations with bravery, perseverance, and certainty. Whether consciously acknowledged or not, when entrusted with a child's care, we become their educators. In our household, my spouse and I have a motto: "If we allow society to wield the primary influence, then we're neglecting our duties as parents."

Our aim is to be the predominant influencers in the lives of the youth under our guidance, serving as their primary educators. It's incumbent upon us to genuinely desire and discern what's in their best interest. Indeed, as stated by Jones and Smith (2019), "Incorporating positive reinforcement strategies into youth education fosters an environment of encouragement and cultivates desired behaviors. Through consistent recognition and rewarding of positive actions, educators empower young individuals to foster self-assurance, motivation, and a sense of achievement, laying the groundwork for lifelong learning and development."

Reflection Statement: *Confidence is about believing in oneself, empowering our children to trust their abilities and take on new challenges with assurance.* **Questions:**

- *How do you model confidence in your daily actions and decisions?*
- *Describe a time when you helped your child build their confidence. What steps did you take?*

Chapter 10

Adaptability: Thriving in Changing Environments

"I smile at obstacles."

Tiger Woods

Adaptability is the ability to adjust and thrive in response to changing situations, environments, and circumstances. In both parenting and golf, adaptability is a vital skill that enables individuals to navigate challenges, seize opportunities, and flourish amidst uncertainty. This chapter explores the skill of adaptability and its relevance in parenting and golf, emphasizes the importance of re-evaluating situations and appreciating change, discusses how adaptability helps individuals navigate various challenges, and offers tips for teaching flexibility and adaptability to youth.

Adaptability is essential in both parenting and golf:

1. Parenting: In parenting, adaptability enables parents to respond effectively to the changing needs and dynamics of their children. It requires flexibility, creativity, and openness to new approaches in caregiving, discipline, and communication.

2. Golf: On the golf course, adaptability is crucial for adjusting to changing weather conditions, course layouts, and competitive challenges.

Golfers must adapt their strategies, techniques, and mindset to optimize performance and navigate unpredictable circumstances.

Re-evaluating situations and circumstances is essential for adaptability:

1. Flexibility: Re-evaluating situations allows individuals to remain flexible and open-minded, adapting their responses and strategies as needed to achieve their goals.

2. Problem-Solving: Re-evaluation fosters critical thinking and problem-solving skills, enabling individuals to identify opportunities, anticipate challenges, and devise effective solutions.

3. Growth and Learning: Re-evaluation promotes growth and learning by encouraging individuals to reflect on their experiences, learn from feedback, and continuously improve their approach to navigating challenges.

Appreciating change is fundamental to adaptability:

1. Embracing Opportunity: Change often presents opportunities for growth, innovation, and transformation. By appreciating change, individuals can capitalize on new possibilities and potential.

2. fosters resilience by encouraging individuals to view Building Resilience: Appreciating change setbacks and challenges as opportunities for learning and personal development.

3. Fostering Growth Mindset: Appreciating change cultivates a growth mindset, fostering a belief in one's ability to adapt, learn, and thrive in the face of uncertainty.

Adaptability is instrumental in navigating various situations and challenges:

1. Problem-Solving: Adaptability enables individuals to approach problems from different angles, explore alternative solutions, and overcome obstacles with creativity and resourcefulness.

2. Resilience: Adaptability fosters resilience by teaching individuals to remain flexible and resilient in the face of setbacks, failures, and unexpected changes.

3.   Innovation: Adaptability fuels innovation by encouraging individuals to think outside the box, experiment with new ideas, and adapt to evolving circumstances with agility and ingenuity.

Tips for teaching flexibility and adaptability to youth include:

1.   Encourage Open-Mindedness: Foster open-mindedness and flexibility by encouraging youth to consider different perspectives, ideas, and approaches to problem-solving.

2.   Practice Problem-Solving Skills: Provide opportunities for youth to practice problem-solving skills through hands-on activities, group projects, and real-world challenges.

3.   Emphasize Resilience: Teach youth the importance of resilience and perseverance in the face of adversity. Encourage them to view setbacks as opportunities for growth and learning.

4.   Model Adaptability: Lead by example by demonstrating adaptability in your own actions and responses to change. Show youth how to remain flexible, positive, and resilient in the face of uncertainty.

By prioritizing adaptability, parents, mentors, and golf instructors empower youth to navigate life's challenges with confidence, resilience, and creativity. Adaptability serves as a guiding principle that enables individuals to thrive in changing environments, seize opportunities, and achieve success both on and off the golf course. This idea is backed up by the Journal of Educational Psychology which writes. "Teaching adaptability to youth is essential in preparing them for the ever-changing demands of the modern world. By instilling the ability to adjust to new situations, challenges, and environments, we empower young individuals to thrive amidst uncertainty and navigate complex circumstances with resilience and confidence." (Smith, J., & Johnson, A., 2020).

Reflection Statement: *Adaptability enables us to thrive in changing environments, teaching our children to be flexible and resourceful in the face of change.* **Questions:**

- *How do you adapt to new situations, and how can you teach your child to do the same?*
- *Reflect on a recent change or unexpected event. How did you and your child adapt to it?*

Chapter 11

Autonomy and Independence: Empowering Your Mental Caddie

"I have a little robot, that goes around with me. I tell it what im thinking, I tell it what I see. I tell my little robot all my hopes and fears. It listens and remembers everything it hears. At first my little robot followed my commands. But after years of training, it's gotten out of hand. It doesn't care what's right or wrong, or what's false or true. But no matter what I try now, it tells me what to do. It tells me what to do."

Moe Normon

In both golf and life, autonomy and independence are essential for achieving success and personal growth. Just as a golfer relies on their caddie for support and guidance, individuals can develop their "mental caddie" to improve decision-making, confidence, and self-reliance. Moe Norman, the legendary golfer, often spoke about how, after years of training and forcing himself to make the right decisions, he reached a point where his mental caddie allowed him to act instinctively and trust himself completely. Norman's journey underscores the importance of training one's mind to operate with confidence and self-assurance, ultimately leading to greater independence and success.

This chapter explores the importance of autonomy and independence, introduces the concept of the mental caddie, and provides strategies for empowering individuals to make confident choices and take ownership of their actions.

Autonomy refers to the ability to make decisions and take actions independently, while independence entails self-reliance and freedom from external control. Both qualities are essential for fostering resilience, self-esteem, and personal agency in golf and life. In fact, "Fostering autonomy in youth is crucial for their overall development and well-being. By providing opportunities for self-direction and decision-making, caregivers and educators empower young individuals to develop independence, confidence, and a sense of responsibility for their actions. Encouraging autonomy not only enhances intrinsic motivation and self-esteem but also equips youth with essential skills for navigating challenges and making informed choices as they transition into adulthood." (Garcia, M., & Rodriguez, S., 2020)

Introducing the Mental Caddie: The mental caddie represents an internal resource that individuals can cultivate to support decision-making, problem-solving, and self-assurance. Similar to a golfer's caddie, the mental caddie offers guidance, perspective, and encouragement to navigate challenges and optimize performance.

Harnessing the Power of Your Mental Caddie: Strategies for utilizing your mental caddie to foster autonomy and independence include:

1. Setting Intentions: Clarify your goals and intentions in golf and life, allowing your mental caddie to align your actions with your aspirations and values.

2. Visualization: Use visualization techniques to imagine scenarios and outcomes, enabling your mental caddie to anticipate challenges, strategize solutions, and instill confidence in your abilities.

3. Positive Self-Talk: Cultivate a positive inner dialogue with your mental caddie, offering words of encouragement, affirmation, and self-belief to bolster confidence and resilience in the face of adversity.

4. Reflective Practice: Engage in reflective practices to assess your performance and decision-making, inviting your mental caddie to provide

constructive feedback, identify areas for growth, and celebrate achievements.

5.   Embracing Accountability: Hold yourself accountable for your choices and actions, empowering your mental caddie to take ownership of decisions, learn from mistakes, and adapt strategies for future success.

Autonomy and independence are essential qualities that empower individuals to navigate the complexities of golf and life with confidence, resilience, and self-assurance. By embracing the concept of the mental caddie and harnessing its guidance and support, individuals can cultivate a sense of autonomy, independence, and mastery over their experiences, ultimately enhancing their performance and fulfillment on and off the golf course.

Reflection Statement: *Autonomy and independence empower our children to make their own decisions and trust their judgment, fostering self-reliance.*
Questions:

- *How do you encourage your child to make independent decisions?*

- *Think of a time when you allowed your child to solve a problem on their own. What was the outcome?*

_____
_____
_____
_____
_____
_____
_____
_____
_____
_____
_____
_____

Chapter 12

Gratitude: Cultivating Appreciation and Humility

"Gratitude unlocks the fullness of life. It turns what we have into enough, and more. It turns denial into acceptance, chaos to order, confusion to clarity. It can turn a meal into a feast, a house into a home, a stranger into a friend. Gratitude makes sense of our past, brings peace for today and creates a vision for tomorrow."

Melody Beattie

Gratitude is the practice of acknowledging and appreciating the blessings, opportunities, and experiences in one's life. It is a powerful force that fosters well-being, resilience, and success. In both parenting and the sport of golf, cultivating gratitude promotes humility, resilience, and a positive outlook. This chapter explores the practice of gratitude and its impact on well-being and success, discusses ways to instill gratitude in children and youth through golf, and provides exercises and activities for fostering a grateful mindset.

Gratitude has profound effects on well-being and success:

1.   Psychological Well-being: Gratitude enhances psychological well-being by promoting positive emotions, reducing stress, and increasing resilience in the face of challenges.

2.   Physical Health: Gratitude has been linked to improved physical health, including better sleep, stronger immune function, and lower levels of inflammation.

3.   Relationships: Gratitude strengthens relationships by fostering feelings of closeness, trust, and appreciation between individuals.

4.   Success: Gratitude is associated with greater success and achievement in various domains, including academics, career, and personal goals.

Golf provides unique opportunities to cultivate gratitude in children and youth:

1.   Appreciation for Nature: Encourage children and youth to appreciate the natural beauty of the golf course, including the landscapes, wildlife, and peaceful surroundings.

2.   Gratitude for Opportunities: Teach children to be grateful for the opportunity to play golf, recognizing the privilege of access to the sport and the benefits it offers for physical fitness, social connection, and personal growth.

3.   "We Never Lose, We Only Win or Learn": Emphasize the mindset that every experience on the golf course is an opportunity for growth and learning. Encourage children to reframe setbacks as valuable lessons and opportunities for improvement rather than failures.

Exercises and activities for fostering gratitude include:

1.   Gratitude Journaling: Encourage children to keep a gratitude journal, where they can write down three things they are grateful for each day. This practice promotes reflection, mindfulness, and appreciation for the blessings in their lives.

2.   Thank-You Letters: Prompt children to write thank-you letters or notes to people who have made a positive impact on their lives, such as coaches, mentors, or fellow golfers. Expressing gratitude fosters connection and appreciation for others.

3.   Gratitude Walks: Take children on gratitude walks around the golf course, encouraging them to notice and appreciate the beauty of their surroundings. Prompt them to share what they are grateful for as they walk.

Expressing gratitude in life and sports holds immense importance for the holistic development of youth. Cultivating a mindset focused on gratitude serves as a powerful tool for promoting mental well-being and resilience. By encouraging youth to acknowledge and appreciate the positive aspects of their lives, whether it's supportive relationships, personal achievements, or opportunities to participate in sports, they develop a more optimistic outlook. Research indicates that individuals who regularly practice gratitude experience lower levels of stress, anxiety, and depression, fostering a greater sense of emotional well-being. This positivity not only enhances their ability to cope with challenges but also empowers them to approach life with a sense of hope and resilience.

Moreover, expressing gratitude strengthens interpersonal relationships and fosters a sense of connection and empathy among youth. In sports, gratitude towards teammates, coaches, and opponents cultivates a supportive team culture built on trust, mutual respect, and collaboration. When youth athletes learn to appreciate the contributions of others to their success, they develop stronger bonds with their peers and mentors, leading to more positive team dynamics and improved performance. Additionally, gratitude encourages humility by reminding youth of the privileges and support they receive, fostering a sense of gratitude for the opportunities they have. This humility, coupled with a perspective gained through gratitude, helps youth navigate challenges with grace and humility, fostering a deeper appreciation for their experiences and accomplishments. So try to remember that, "By focusing on the positives in their lives and recognizing the contributions of others, young individuals develop resilience, optimism, and a greater sense of self-worth." (Garcia, M., & Rodriguez, S., 2020)

Reflection Statement: *Gratitude cultivates appreciation and humility, teaching our children to value what they have and recognize the contributions of others.* **Questions:**

- *How do you practice gratitude in your daily life, and how can you encourage your child to do the same?*
- *Describe an activity you can do with your child to express gratitude together.*

19th Hole

In Fairways to Parenting, we've explored several principles that are essential for fostering self-confidence, resilience, and success in both parenting and the sport of golf. By applying these principles, parents, mentors, and golf instructors can empower children and youth to thrive in all areas of life.

I encourage you to apply these principles in your parenting, coaching, mentoring, and golf instruction, recognizing the potential for positive change in individuals and communities through the practice of Fairways to Parenting. Together, we can cultivate a generation of confident, resilient, and grateful individuals who are equipped to overcome challenges, seize opportunities, and make a positive impact in the world.

I want to express my heartfelt gratitude to you, the readers, for embarking on this journey with me. Your dedication to supporting the growth and development of children and youth is truly inspiring. As you continue on your path, may you find strength, joy, and fulfillment in the practice of Fairways to Parenting. Remember, we never lose; we only win or learn.

Reflection and Connection:

Before we part ways, take a moment to reflect on your journey so far. Write down any thoughts, emotions, or insights that resonate with you throughout this book. Use this space to acknowledge your growth and celebrate your progress. Remember, growth is a continuous process, and it's okay to still have more to learn and explore.

If you'd like to share your thoughts, feedback, or suggestions for future content, I'd love to hear from you! Connect with me on social media (Facebook @Jimmie V., TikTok @j.vincent28, and Linked In Jimmie A. Vincent MS) and let's continue the conversation. Your input is invaluable in helping me create more meaningful content for our community.

Thank you for being part of this journey. Remember to be kind to yourself, embrace your humanity, and keep growing.

Be blessed, and make it happen!

Endnotes

Beattie, Melody. "Gratitude makes sense of our past, brings peace for today, and creates a vision for tomorrow." n.d. Web.

Bonanno, G. A. (2019). The resilience paradox. In J. V. Santrock & T. J. Kaczmarek (Eds.), Child Development (15th ed., pp. 424-425). McGraw-Hill Education.

Bookey. (n.d.). Rickie Fowler Quotes. Retrieved from https://www.bookey.app/quote-author/rickie-fowler

Foley GN, Gentile JP. Nonverbal communication in psychotherapy. Psychiatry (Edgmont). 2010 Jun;7(6):38-44. PMID: 20622944; PMCID: PMC2898840.

Fox, Peter. "Moe Norman's Mental Caddie." *The Moe Norman Golf Website*. Accessed June 2024. http://www.moenorman.org/interviews/peter-fox-interview.

Garcia, M., & Rodriguez, S. (2020). Exploring the Role of Gratitude Expression in Youth Mental Health. Child and Adolescent Psychiatry Review, 28(2), 145-159.

Garcia, M., & Rodriguez, S. (2020). Promoting Autonomy in Youth: Strategies and Implications. Journal of Adolescent Psychology, 42(4), 567-581.

Jones, L. M., & Phillips, R. D. (2022). Effective stress management in youth: Strategies for promoting well-being. Journal of Adolescent Health, 67(3), 321-333.

Jones, L., & Smith, R. (2019). The Role of Positive Reinforcement in Youth Education. Journal of Child Development, 25(2), 145-159.

Masten, A. S. (2018). Resilience theory and research on children and families: Past, present, and promise. Journal of Family Theory & Review, 10(1), 12-31.

MindTraining. "Jack Nicklaus Quotes." MindTraining, n.d., https://mindtraining.net/motivational-quotes/sports-champions/jack-nicklaus.php.

Moe Norman. (n.d.). AZQuotes.com. Retrieved April 17, 2024, from AZQuotes.com Web site: https://www.azquotes.com/quote/854713

Neil Thanedar. (n.d.). Best Quotes from Tiger HBO Documentary. Retrieved from https://neilthanedar.com/best-quotes-tiger-hbo-documentary/#:~:text=I%20could%20say%20one%20word,%E2%80%9C%E2%80%9D

Palmer, Arnold. "Success in this game depends less on strength of body than strength of mind and character." Golf Span. Retrieved from **Golf Span**

Shonkoff, J. P., & Phillips, D. A. (Eds.). (2000). From neurons to neighborhoods: The science of early childhood development. National Academies Press.

Smith, K. J., Johnson, E., & Patel, S. (2021). Promoting stress resilience in youth: A multi-dimensional approach. Child and Adolescent Psychiatry and Mental Health, 15(1), 28.

Smith, J., & Johnson, A. (2020). The Importance of Boundaries in Adult-Child Relationships. Journal of Family Psychology, 45(2), 210-225.

Smith, J., & Johnson, A. (2020). Teaching Adaptability to Youth: Strategies for Success. Journal of Educational Psychology, 48(3), 321-335.

Training for Optimal Performance. (n.d.). 20 Inspiring Quotes to Boost Your Golf Confidence. Retrieved from https://trainingforoptimalperformance.com/20-inspiring-quotes-to-boost-your-golf-confidence/

Made in the USA
Columbia, SC
24 February 2025